Decodable Stories
Takehome Books

Grade 3

McGraw Hill Education

Bothell, WA • Chicago, IL • Columbus, OH • New York, NY

MHEonline.com

Send all inquiries to:
McGraw-Hill Education
8787 Orion Place
Columbus, OH 43240

ISBN: 978-0-07-671149-9
MHID: 0-07-671149-8

Printed in the United States of America.

8 9 10 LMN 22 21 20

Contents

About the Decodable Stories Takehome Books

The **SRA Open Court Reading** *Decodable Stories Takehome Books* allow your students to apply their knowledge of phonic elements to read simple, engaging texts. Each story supports instruction in a new phonic element and incorporates elements and words that have been learned earlier.

The students can fold and staple the pages of each *Decodable Story Takehome Book* to make books of their own to keep and read. We suggest that you keep extra sets of the stories in your classroom for the children to reread.

How to Make a Takehome Book

1. Tear out the pages you need.

2. Place the title page facedown and the page with two consecutive folios (pages 4–5 in example) faceup.

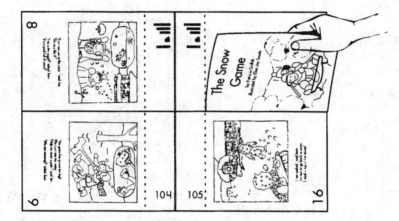

For 16-page book

3. Place the pages on top of each other in order. The facedown title page will be on the bottom, and the page with the consecutive folios (pages 8–9 in example) will be faceup on the top.

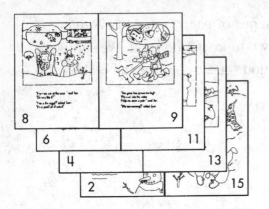

4. Fold along the center line.

5. Check to make sure the pages are in order.

6. Staple the pages along the fold.

For 8-page book

3. Place the page with consecutive folios (page 4–5 in example) on top of the other page.

4. Fold along the center line.

5. Check to make sure the pages are in order.

6. Staple the pages along the fold.

Just to let you know...

A message from _____

    Help your child discover the joy of independent reading with *SRA Open Court Reading*. From time to time your child will bring home his or her very own *Decodable Stories Takehome Books* to share with you. With your help, these stories can give your child important reading practice and a joyful shared reading experience.

    You may want to set aside a few minutes every evening to read these stories together. Here are some suggestions you may find helpful:

- Do not expect your child to read each story perfectly, but concentrate on sharing the book together.
- Participate by doing some of the reading.
- Talk about the stories as you read, give lots of encouragement, and watch as your child becomes more fluent throughout the year!

    Learning to read takes lots of practice. Sharing these stories is one way that your child can gain that valuable practice. Encourage your child to keep the *Decodable Stories Takehome Books* in a special place. This collection will make a library of books that your child can read and reread. Take the time to listen to your child read from his or her library. Just a few moments of shared reading each day can give your child the confidence needed to excel in reading.

    Children who read every day come to think of reading as a pleasant, natural part of life. One way to inspire your child to read is to show that reading is an important part of your life by letting him or her see you reading books, magazines, newspapers, or any other materials. Another good way to show that you value reading is to share a *Decodable Story Takehome Book* with your child each day.

    Successful reading experiences allow children to be proud of their new-found reading ability. Support your child with interest and enthusiasm about reading. You won't regret it!

Midge

by Sarah Thompson
illustrated by Meryl Henderson

Decodable Story 3

Mc Graw Hill Education

Bothell, WA • Chicago, IL • Columbus, OH • New York, NY

MHEonline.com

Mc Graw Hill Education

Copyright © 2015 McGraw-Hill Education

Send all inquiries to:
McGraw-Hill Education
8787 Orion Place
Columbus, OH 43240

Midge is a big dog with a big head. Jack walks Midge. But Midge is too big! Midge walks Jack!

Next, Quinn helps. Now Midge walks. Good job, Quinn! Midge is a big dog. Six children must walk her Midge!

Midge tugs Jack into plants. Can Jack get help?
Liz helps. Liz and Jack move Midge from the plants.

Frank helps. Midge stops for a second. But just a second.
Then Midge jumps and sniffs a bug. The kids jump as
well!

The twins run and help.
bridge. Help!
But big Midge yanks Liz and Jack. She yanks them to a

But Midge springs up. The children spring with Midge!
Jack, Liz, and the twins move big Midge back.

Tell Your Pals

by Olivia Herzog

illustrated by Meryl Henderson

Decodable Story 4

Bothell, WA • Chicago, IL • Columbus, OH • New York, NY

MHEonline.com

Send all inquiries to:
McGraw-Hill Education
8787 Orion Place
Columbus, OH 43240

The kids looked sore and worn out. Midge did not.
"Fran, tell your pals Midge's story last!" Mom grinned.
"I will," Fran grinned back.

Mom and Fran sat in the yard. "School starts soon," said
Mom.
"Yes," nodded Fran. "I will see school pals."

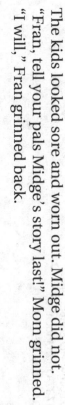

23

Midge ran in Fran's yard. "Do not harm Fran's corn!" yelled Mom.

The kids yanked barking Midge from Fran's dirt.

30

Mom spotted Fran's big garden. "Tell about planting corn."

"I will not forget," said Fran. "Digging up earth was hard."

27

"And tell about the park," Mom said.
"We had fun! I hit! I ran! I scored runs!" grinned Fran.

Fran heard barking. "It's Midge!" yelled Fran.
Fran spotted a blur. Midge ran fast from the corner.
More than six kids ran with her.

Stars

by Liam Miller

illustrated by Meryl Henderson

Decodable Story 5

Mc Graw Hill Education

Bothell, WA • Chicago, IL • Columbus, OH • New York, NY

MHEonline.com

Mc Graw Hill Education

Send all inquiries to:
McGraw-Hill Education
8787 Orion Place
Columbus, OH 43240

Chip sat on a short bench in his yard. He had a chart with him.
His chart had stars marked on it.

"A jet?" Josh asked.
"A jet is not on this chart," was Chip's answer.
The pals grinned.

It was a dark night. Chip used his chart to spot a lot of stars.

The stars looked like sparks burning in the night.

Another flash of light shot in a path far above them. Chip turned and grabbed Josh's shirt. "What was that?" Chip asked.

Josh visited that night. Josh was Chip's friend. Josh sat on the bench and watched the stars with Chip.

A light flashed above them in a blur. It shocked Chip and Josh.
"That was fast!" yelled Josh.

Val's New Bike

by Daniel Fairwood
illustrated by Kersti Frigell

Decodable Story 6

Bothell, WA • Chicago, IL • Columbus, OH • New York, NY

MHEonline.com

Send all inquiries to:
McGraw-Hill Education
8787 Orion Place
Columbus, OH 43240

29

Val got a new bike for her birthday! On the bike, above the back tire, there was a plate. It had Val's name on it. Val admired that the most.

"I thought I would find it," said Val. "Thanks, Vic! Sorry I cannot talk. It is time for me to ride home." Val smiled as she rode her bike back home.

Val did not postpone riding her bike. She rode to Vic's home first. Vic was standing in his garden, next to the back gate.

Val rode back to Vic's. Vic spotted Val and came running. "Val! Your nameplate fell by my gate," Vic said. He gave the plate to Val.

"Hi, Vic!" said Val. "What are you doing?"
"I have chores to do in the garden," said Vic. Then Vic spotted Val's new bike. "Great bike, Val!"

Val smiled. "I will ride the same way home. I hope I can find it."
"That is a fine thought," said Kate.

33

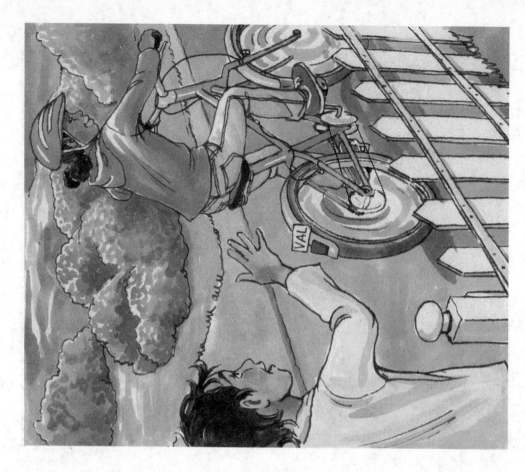

Vic came down for a look at Val's bike.

"This is a fine bike," said Vic. "I like this nameplate over the tire!"

Val smiled and thanked Vic, then rode from the gate.

"Where did it go?" asked Val.

"Did it come off on your ride?" asked Kate.

Next Val stopped at Cal's home. "It looks like it can go fast," said Cal. "Perhaps you can finish first for a change."

6

Val looked by the tire. The plate was not there!

11

"It is fast, but it has good brakes," said Val.
"Good, that helps make it safe," said Cal.

"That is kind," said Val. "I like the nameplate the most."
"What nameplate?" asked Kate.

The last stop on Val's ride was Kate's yard.
Val hoped Kate would like the new bike.

Kate was reading in the shade when Val rode up.
"Hello, Val, great new bike," said Kate.

Vic's Big Chore

by Katherine Burke

illustrated by Kersti Frigell

Decodable Story 7

Bothell, WA • Chicago, IL • Columbus, OH • New York, NY

MHEonline.com

Send all inquiries to:
McGraw-Hill Education
8787 Orion Place
Columbus, OH 43240

Val hit the brakes. She jumped off her bike. "Vic," she yelled. "Let's go for a ride!" Vic was in his garden.

Val sped off. Vic jumped on his bike. He chased after Val. "Hold up!" yelled Vic. "Pals compete with pals," Val yelled back.

"I cannot yet," said Vic. "I must finish my chores."
Val smiled. "I did mine this morning," she said.

Vic said, "Thanks, Val. I am grateful for your help."
"Pals help pals," smiled Val.
Val jumped on her bike.

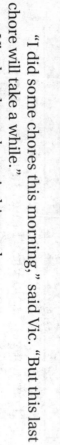

"I did some chores this morning," said Vic. "But this last chore will take a while."

Vic then bent down in his garden.

Soon the pile of clover was high, and there was no clover in the garden!

"Time to ride!" said Val.

41

Vic gave Val a quick lesson. Vic instructed Val in the basics of hand-pulling clover. "Yank close to the bottom," he told her.

Val pulled clover. Vic pulled clover. Clover fell.

Val watched Vic. He used his hands to pull high green plants in the garden. The plants had little white blossoms on them.

"I see those plants all over. They are hard to ignore," said Val.

"These are white clover plants," said Vic.

"They look cute," said Val.

"You want to help?" Vic reacted in shock.

"I want to ride bikes," said Val. "So I would like you to finish fast."

Vic smiled.

43

"Five or six plants can look fine," said Vic. "But hundreds in a garden do not. They look boring!"
Val looked. "That is so," she said.

Vic made a pile of clover plants. Val watched a bit. Then she asked, "Can I help you?"

"And high white clover shades other plants. Those plants cannot get big then," added Vic.
He used both his hands to pull the white clover.

"You are a secret clover expert," said Val.
"No, my mom is," grinned Vic. "I am a clover puller."
As he spoke, Vic grabbed more clover.

Gem Is Missing

by Curtis Brinkman

illustrated by Kersti Frigell

Decodable Story 8

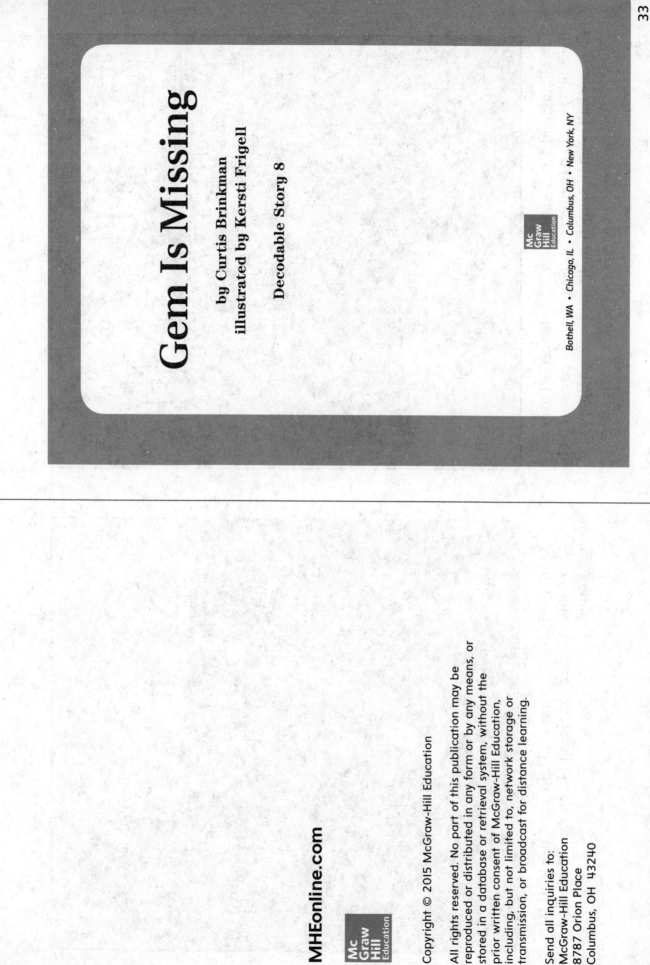

Bothell, WA • Chicago, IL • Columbus, OH • New York, NY

Mc Graw Hill Education

MHEonline.com

Mc Graw Hill Education

Send all inquiries to:
McGraw-Hill Education
8787 Orion Place
Columbus, OH 43240

Ginger and Mom walked fast. They looked all over as they did. They had to find Gem. Gem was the name of their dog. She had been missing from home for some time.

Mom ran in the high clover. There sat little Gem. In seconds, Ginger had Gem in her arms. The little dog made it home!

Ginger and Mom lived in a place named Old Glen Crossing. Once, this land had been filled with things like farms, barns, and fences.

47

On the porch, Mom heard a soft yelp. "What is that?" she asked.

Ginger heard it too. "It is Gem!" yelled Ginger.

Now Old Glen Crossing was filled with homes. Around them was open space. Ponds, plants, and cinder paths filled the space.

Sad Gem heard the kids. But she could not see them. She was in too much high white clover! Little Gem started to yelp.

"Gem!" yelled Ginger and Mom. Vic and Val went racing past. They lived at Old Glen Crossing, too. They heard Ginger and her mom.

The kids sat on Ginger's porch. They sat in a circle. They suggested places Gem could be. Mom made notes.

"We will help find Gem," Val said. Soon more kids helped. But no one spotted little Gem. Ginger felt sad.

It was hot. Mom and Ginger felt tired. The kids felt tired. "Let's go home," said Mom. "We can think about places to find Gem. We can exchange ideas."

"Mom, we will never find Gem," said Ginger.
"I think we will," hoped Mom.
Ginger hoped that as well.

51

Mom and Ginger felt that Gem was far away. They did not hunt close to home. They hunted in deserted places at Old Glen Crossing.

Old Glen Crossing was large. It had much space to hide in. But Gem did not want to hide. She wanted to go to her bed.

Yet Gem was not far away! She sat in high white clover in her yard! The clover looked like a giant fence to Gem.

On a Train

by Helen Garcia
illustrated by Kersti Frigell

Decodable Story 9

Mc Graw Hill Education

Bothell, WA • Chicago, IL • Columbus, OH • New York, NY

MHEonline.com

Mc Graw Hill Education

Send all inquiries to:
McGraw-Hill Education
8787 Orion Place
Columbus, OH 43240

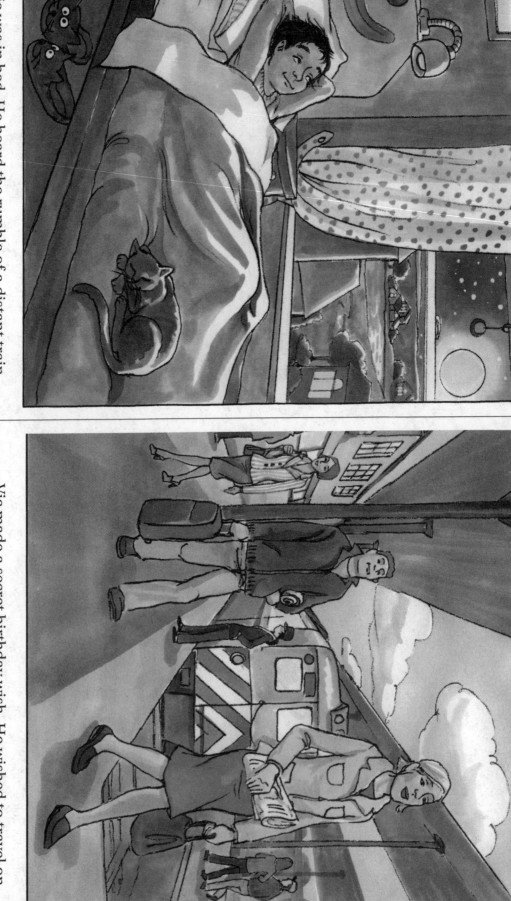

Vic was in bed. He heard the rumble of a distant train. Old Glen Crossing's name came from trains. Two metal train tracks crossed very close by.

Vic made a secret birthday wish. He wished to travel on trains to all those places. It was a fun wish. It was a very fun day.

54

Trains had used those tracks for a long time. Some trains took cargo across the USA. Other trains let people travel from city to city.

55

Vic and pals walked around and looked at more trains. Each train was going to a different city. Some places were far, far away.

Vic liked that he could hear trains. He liked hearing the trains clicking on the tracks. Trains made Vic picture faraway places.

Soon the train was in the city. It made city stops, as well. Its last stop was the best. It was in the middle of the city.

A train stopped near Old Glen Crossing. Lots of people from Old Glen Crossing rode trains. Some rode them every day.

53

The train made lots of stops. At each stop, riders got on and off, but Vic stayed on. Vic liked seeing the face of each person.

60

57

But Vic had never been on a train. That was going to change. Mom and Dad had a surprise for him.

A conductor came through the train. She checked tickets. She checked Vic, Val, and Ray's tickets. Vic planned to save his ticket.

59

For his birthday, Mom and Dad were taking Vic on a train ride. The ride was into the city. And Vic got to bring Val and Ray.

Vic felt surprised at how quiet it was in the racing train. He could hear it clicking on the metal tracks. But it was gentle.

Vic, Val, and Ray sat in the train. So did Vic's mom and dad. Vic felt excited. He was traveling on a train at last!

When the big train first started, it did not go fast. But it sped up quick. After a short time, it was zipping past tranquil farms for grain and ranches for cattle and other animals.

Bike Races

by Curtis Brinkman
illustrated by Kersti Frigell

Decodable Story 10

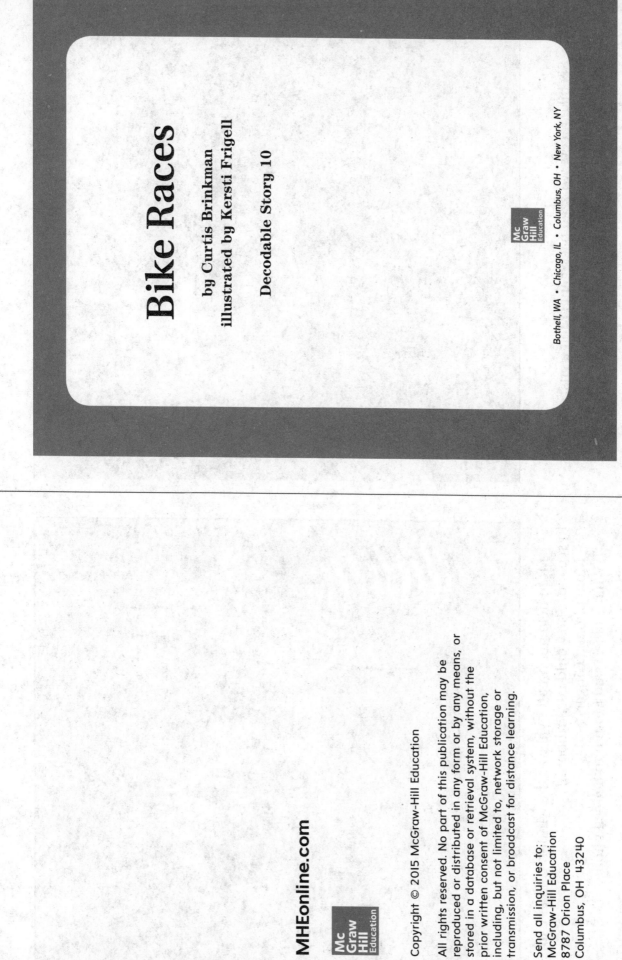

Mc Graw Hill Education

Bothell, WA • Chicago, IL • Columbus, OH • New York, NY

MHEonline.com

Mc Graw Hill Education

Send all inquiries to:
McGraw-Hill Education
8787 Orion Place
Columbus, OH 43240

Six bike racers whizzed past. Ginger felt a gust. The bikes were going that fast!
"What a race!" said Ginger into her cell phone.

Mom held her breath. Val was the winner. Ginger came in second. She would get a ribbon!
Mom phoned Ginger.
"What a race!" said Mom into her cell phone.

Ginger was watching the Old Glen Crossing Bike Races. For years, these races have happened every summer. There were races for adults and kids.

The three girls raced past yelling pals. Vic and Ray felt a rush when the bikes knifed past the finish line. Which was the winner?

Most races were for adults. Riders competed for medals and cash prizes. Riders came from all over for those races.

At the top of the hill, Val, Steph, and Ginger were in first place.
The last phase was flat. Riders had to pump hard.

65

Some races were for kids. Winners did not get cash or medals. Kids got ribbons.

Ginger was going to ride in the girls' race soon.

Going down, most of the racing opponents stayed close to each other.

The middle phase was harder. It was an uphill climb.

"Are you as excited as I am for the ride, Ginger?" asked Mom. Mom was also on a cell phone. Mom was rushing to Ginger's race.

Ginger and ten other girls pedaled fast. Ginger's legs pumped high.

The first phase of this race was not hard. It was down a hill.

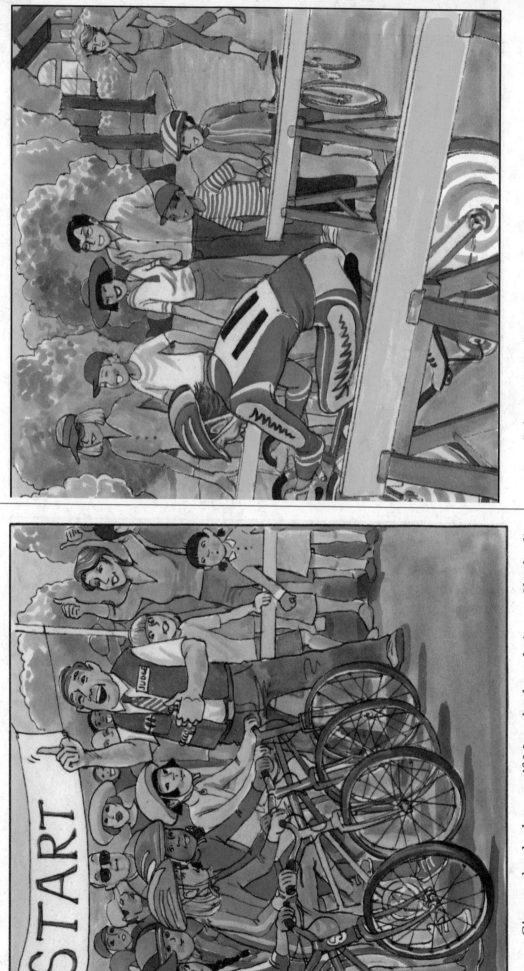

67

Ginger checked to see if Mom had made it yet. She had! Mom gave Ginger a thumbs–up for luck.

A judge yelled, "Go!"

"I know I am," Ginger responded.

Ginger was standing next to her bike. She had on her helmet. She glanced at the watch on her wrist.

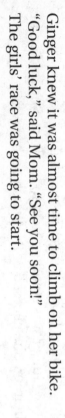

Ginger knew it was almost time to climb on her bike.
"Good luck," said Mom. "See you soon!"
The girls' race was going to start.

Ginger stuck the phone in her pocket. Moments later, she was at the starting line. Ginger was filled with strength!

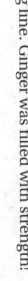

68

Too Cold?

by Katherine Burke

illustrated by Kersti Frigell

Decodable Story 11

Mc Graw Hill Education

Bothell, WA • Chicago, IL • Columbus, OH • New York, NY

MHEonline.com

Mc Graw Hill Education

Send all inquiries to:
McGraw-Hill Education
8787 Orion Place
Columbus, OH 43240

It was winter in Old Glen Crossing. The air was cold, and the land had a tranquil white blanket over it. There was too much ice, for bike travel now.

"No," chuckled Ray with humor. "I am too hot!" The pals looked at Ray. He had lots of clothes and blankets on him. He was too hot!

Still there was a lot for the pals to do. In fact, this was the Winter Festival. This was such an exciting time!

The final event was the bonfire.
"I do not think I can go," Ray told his pals.
"What's wrong?" Val asked. "Too cold?"

The weather was cold. Most kids felt the weather was perfect for the Festival. But Ray did not. He felt too cold!

Ray's pals saw that Ray felt cold. They wanted to help him. Ray's pals gave Ray mittens, scarves, hats, jackets, blankets, and thick winter pants.

Next was a sports match. The winning side would get a prize. Ray did not compete. He was a fan. He was a frozen fan!

The first Winter Festival event was ice-skating. The pals raced and twirled circles on the ice, but Ray just shivered. His hands felt numb.

"Use these extra mittens," said Val. "Mom knit them for me."

"Thanks," said Ray. He slipped them over his thumbs and knuckles.

"Slide this stocking cap on your head," Steph said. Ray did as he was told. "Thanks, Steph," he said. But Ray still felt cold!

Soon it was sledding time. The pals climbed the giant hill and then whizzed down. Some moms and dads snapped photos of the fun.

"It must have taken lots of detail to generate these," said Ray. He chattered as he spoke. Steph saw that Ray was cold.

Ray sledded, but he was still cold. Vic gave Ray a scarf. "Wrap it around your neck," said Vic. "It will help."

"Thanks a lot," said Ray to Vic.

Now it was time to judge the ice—carving display. Adults did the carving. Kids did the judging.

The Empty Field

by Daniel Fairwood

illustrated by Luanne Martin

Decodable Story 12

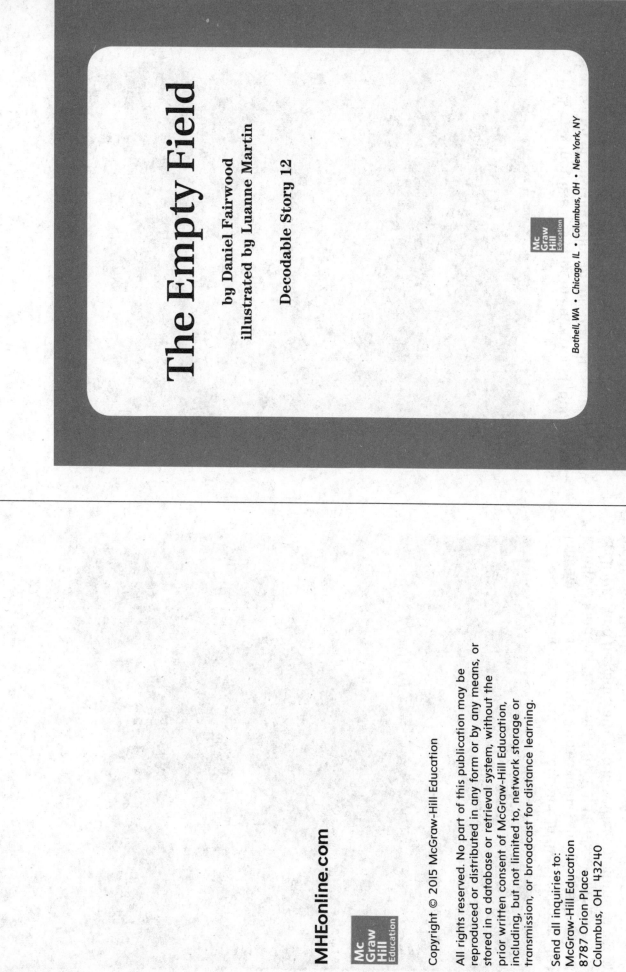

Mc
Graw
Hill
Education

Bothell, WA • Chicago, IL • Columbus, OH • New York, NY

MHEonline.com

Mc
Graw
Hill
Education

Send all inquiries to:
McGraw-Hill Education
8787 Orion Place
Columbus, OH 43240

This may look like it is only an empty field. But it is not. There is a lot of life concealed in this field. It is an important habitat for many plants and animals. Let's go see what we can find.

She also hears an eagle screeching in the air above. He is looking for a tasty snack. The eagle has sharp eyes, but the bunny is hidden. That means the field looks empty to the eagle too, and he glides away to look for something to eat in a different field.

The beehive is in a tree on the border of the field. The bees made their hive in the trunk of a beech tree. The bees return to the hive with pollen for the queen. Other bees buzz nearby.

Dug in beneath the beech tree is a bunny rabbit. Bunnies can hear very well because they have large ears. The bunny can hear the bees buzzing above. But she knows the bees do not want to hurt her.

Can you see this baby deer sleeping in the green grass? His spots help hide him from being seen. He seems at ease, but he knows he must stay ready. He listens closely, and studies each crunch or splash he hears. Is that a nearby stream or an enemy closing in?

It's a wild turkey and her family! The series of chirps and cheeps is coming from her babies. They are not a danger to the deer. The turkeys are only looking for seeds, leaves, and berries to eat. They ignore the baby deer and keep looking for any hidden treats.

Buzzing above the turkey family is a bee. The bee is also looking for something to eat. He spots a large daisy and buzzes close. He will collect pollen and take it back to the queen bee. She is a part of a hive near the edge of the field.

9

Bats

by Curtis Brinkman
illustrated by Meryl Henderson

Decodable Story 13

Mc
Graw
Hill
Education

Bothell, WA • Chicago, IL • Columbus, OH • New York, NY

MHEonline.com

Mc
Graw
Hill
Education

Send all inquiries to:
McGraw-Hill Education
8787 Orion Place
Columbus, OH 43240

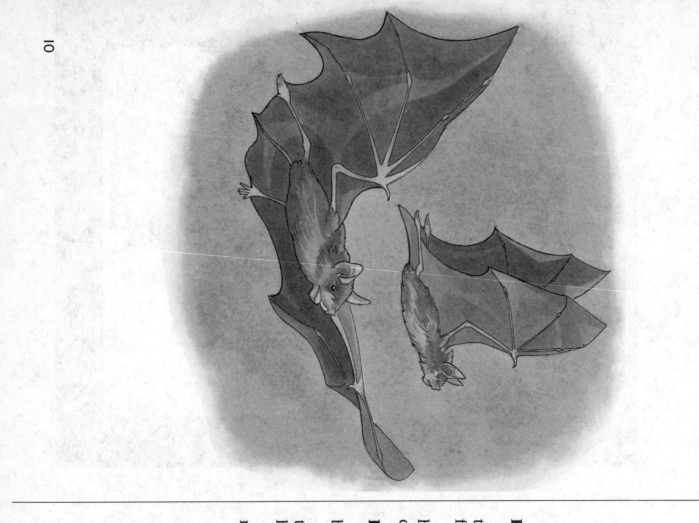

Bats hide well.

Do bats live near you? Bats might, but it is hard to tell. Bats sleep out of sight in daytime. Bats fly and hunt for bugs at night.

Where can bats sleep? Bats can doze in barns, caves, high up in trees, or under bridges. And bats don't lie down to sleep. Bats sleep hanging upside down.

Bats help people and habitats.

People need bats. Why? Bats eat lots of bugs. Some bugs harm farmers' crops.

Bats live in most habitats. And bats help each habitat that they live in. In some places, bats are like bees. Bats help plants survive.

And bats can help you. How? The next story will tell more.

Bats! These strange flying animals frighten some kids and amaze others. One thing is apparent. Not many kids think bats are boring!

Yet, there are things kids do not understand about bats. And some things that kids think about bats are just wrong.

Here are bat facts that you might like to know and share.

Bats are not birds.

Bats fly, so they must be birds. Right? Wrong! Bats are mammals.

- Birds have feathers. Mammals have fur or hair.
- Mammals are born live. Birds hatch from eggs.
- Mammals give milk to their babies. Birds do not.

And birds can fly, but mammals cannot—except for bats! That's why bats are amazing.

Bats are not rodents.

Some kids think of bats as flying rats or mice. Rats and mice are rodents. Rodents are little mammals with strong teeth. Squirrels, beavers, and gophers are rodents, too, but bats are not.

Here is a surprise: Bats are more like apes and chimps than rodents!

Bats are not blind.

You may have heard the phrase, "as blind as a bat." Yet bats are not blind. Bats see well. But bats also send invisible waves as they fly. These waves reflect off things. These waves help bats find and catch insects at night. For bats, these waves are even better than sight!

More Bats

by Ella Cherup
illustrated by Meryl Henderson

Decodable Story 14

Mc
Graw
Hill
Education

Bothell, WA • Chicago, IL • Columbus, OH • New York, NY

MHEonline.com

Mc
Graw
Hill
Education

Send all inquiries to:
McGraw-Hill Education
8787 Orion Place
Columbus, OH 43240

A gentle wind was blowing. "The breeze feels nice," said Cody.

"Yes," agreed Joan. "A breeze after a slow, long rain is refreshing."

Cody and Joan looked at a meadow next to Joan's house. There were little puddles of water here and there.

"But those puddles frighten me a bit," Cody admitted.

"Puddles frighten you? Why?" asked Joan.

"Puddles are places for bugs," said Cody. "Insects lay lots of eggs in puddles. Then more bugs hatch and grow. And the bugs are bad ones. They bite people!"

"I know about bugs and puddles," said Joan. "But the same puddles do not frighten me."

"Why not?" asked Cody.

"My dad made it," Joan said. "He hung it so bats might live here."

Cody was shocked. "Did it work?" he asked.

"Yes," said Joan. "An entire bat colony lives in the box."

"That means loads of bats! Why?" asked Cody. He looked a little afraid. He slowly backed away from the pole.

"Well, do you know what bats eat?" asked Joan.

"No," said Cody.

"Bugs!" smiled Joan. "A bat eats 500 bugs in a short time. A bat colony eats bugs all night."

"Your bats protect you from meadow puddles!" Cody said.

"Yes," said Joan. "Our bats will eat those bugs."

Cody said, "That means I can like bats."

Joan smiled. "Unless you are a bug!" she said.

"I will show you," replied Joan.

Joan led Cody to the side of her house. She showed him an odd–looking box. It was on a pole next to an oak tree. "Do you know what this is?"

"No," said Cody.

"It is a bat box," explained Joan.

"A *bat box*?" said a surprised Cody.

"Yes, it is made from cedar lumber," said Joan. "Bats like cedar."

"Bats!" said Cody. The term stuck in his throat. "You mean those creepy little things with wings?"

Joan smiled. "Yes," she said.

"I know why people have bird houses," said Cody. "But why would you have a bat box?"

Condors

by Ella Cherup
illustrated by Meryl Henderson

Decodable Story 15

Mc Graw Hill Education

Bothell, WA • Chicago, IL • Columbus, OH • New York, NY

MHEonline.com

Mc Graw Hill Education

Copyright © 2015 McGraw-Hill Education

Send all inquiries to:
McGraw-Hill Education
8787 Orion Place
Columbus, OH 43240

That rescue plan continues. Now, in cliffs high in the air, male and female condors sit on eggs and wait for condor babies to hatch. We wait, too. We want condors around for a long time.

This story tells about another animal that helps humans. Without human help, this huge bird would not have survived.

Some people argue that a condor is an ugly–looking bird. Why? It has fluffy feathers all over its body. But its head looks like it has been shaved. That makes a condor's head seem too small. Plus the condor's face is often pink, red, or blue. In the middle of that face is a huge, odd–looking beak.

Yet when a condor flies, people change their minds about its looks. It is the biggest bird in the United States. Its wings stretch nine to ten feet apart. The undersides of its wings are white, outlined by black.

Up in the air, a condor is an incredible sight. It often seems to fly without working at it. It just seems to float.

Yet for a while, not many condors had a chance to live that long. We humans hurt their habitat. We hurt condors. Condors came close to dying out. In the 1980s, just a few of these large birds were left.

Humans harmed condors, but humans also helped them. In the 1980s, a plan was started to rescue condors.

Long ago, people called the condor by another name. They called it the thunderbird. The condor seemed so big that when it flapped its wings, it could make thunder! Few can deny how amazing the thunderbird looks flying high up in the sky. People continue to think that the condor stands for strength.

In its habitat, a condor has real value. A condor does not kill animals to survive. It eats animals that have died! That seems yucky, but it's good. Condors help keep our world clean.

And each condor can help the world for a long time. Some condors live sixty years.

Migrating Geese

by Tony Parker

illustrated by Lynne Avril

Decodable Story 17

Mc Graw Hill Education

Bothell, WA • Chicago, IL • Columbus, OH • New York, NY

MHEonline.com

Mc Graw Hill Education

Send all inquiries to:
McGraw-Hill Education
8787 Orion Place
Columbus, OH 43240

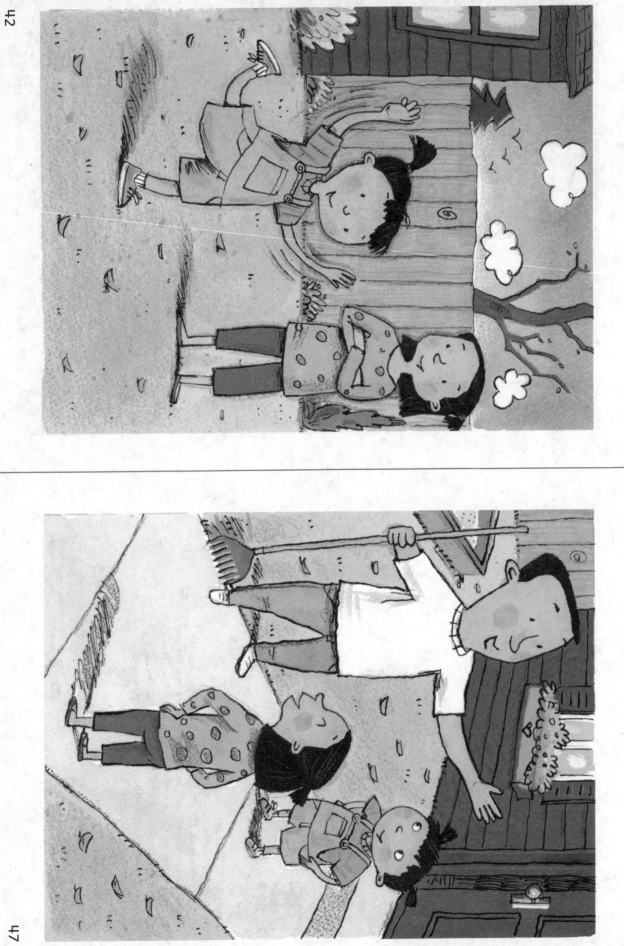

Little Eva began flapping her arms slowly and smoothly. Sue watched her and grinned. "Eva, what are you pretending to be?" she asked.

"I am a goose," said Eva. "I am a goose on the loose!"

"I knew it!" said Sue. She began to flap her arms, too. "I am up in the blue sky, too."

Eva and Sue ran slowly around the yard. They passed the wading pool. Eva nodded to it.

"Do you see the pond below us?" yelled Eva. Sue pretended the pool was a pond. "Yes," she yelled back.

"We just flew from there. It is our summer habitat in a valley. But now we are flying away," Eva told Sue.

"We are flying through a strong storm," yelled Eva. Both girls pretended the storm blew them up and down as they approached it.

Then the girls flew along the sandbox. "See that patch below. It's a desert," yelled Eva.

"Do geese fly over deserts?" asked Sue.

"The truth is that I do not know," said Eva.

The sisters flew past Dad. He smiled. What were they doing? Their flapping arms were a clue. Dad played along. He cried to the girls, "Excuse me, little goofy ducks, but it is noon. It's time for lunch."

Eva stopped flapping. "Dad! We are not goofy ducks. We are goofy geese!" she said.

Sue chuckled. "That is true!"

Dad and Eva chuckled, too.

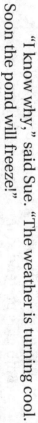

"I know why," said Sue. "The weather is turning cool. Soon the pond will freeze!"

Eva ran fast and zoomed around Sue. She continued flapping her arms. "You are right, Goose Sue," she said. "We are migrating to our winter home."

"How many geese are following us?" asked Sue.

"Quite a few," explained Eva.

The girls ran a bit more. "I am the goose leader!" said Eva. "I rule!"

Sue smiled at her little sister. "Okay. I am following you!"

"We are flying over vast open fields," added Eva. "Let's swoop down for a closer look."

Both girls turned and dipped on one side. Eva led Sue through the garden sprinkler.

A Trade

by Helen Garcia
illustrated by Lynne Avril

Decodable Story 18

Mc
Graw
Hill
Education

Bothell, WA • Chicago, IL • Columbus, OH • New York, NY

MHEonline.com

Mc
Graw
Hill
Education

Send all inquiries to:
McGraw-Hill Education
8787 Orion Place
Columbus, OH 43240

Nathan and Will played video games in the morning. The game they played the most had a superhero called the Blue Hood. He wore a dark blue hood and chased crooks.

Later that afternoon, Nathan and Will played video games again. But this time, Will did not win the Blue Hood game all the time. Now Nathan knew the secret too.

"Nathan!" Will said. "You have a copy of the first Blue Hood comic!"

Before there were Blue Hood video games, there were Blue Hood comic books.

Nathan looked into the wooden box. Then he held up another comic book. "I have *two* copies of the first Blue Hood," he said.

Will was quiet. He seemed to be thinking. Then he said, "I will trade you for one of the copies."

It was Nathan's turn to think. "Will," he said. "I will trade my comic book for the three newest Blue Hood comic books—and for one more thing."

"What?" asked Will.

"The secret to winning the Blue Hood video game!" grinned Nathan.

Both Nathan and Will were good players. But Nathan could never win the Blue Hood game. "I know a secret for winning this game," explained Will.

Nathan stood up and stretched. "I wish I knew the secret," he said.

At noon, the kids took time out to eat. Nathan's mom gave them lunch. They had tuna salad, apples, and wheat crackers.

As Nathan munched a cracker, he said, "I am a bit tired of video games."

"Me too," said Will. "My eyes hurt from looking at the screen."

Nathan had an idea. "Mom," he asked. "Can we look in the attic?"

Nathan watched his mom think. Then she shook her head yes.

"I was going to dust up there," she said. "So you kids can go up with me."

"Thanks!" said Nathan.

Nathan's attic was loaded with stuff. Nathan's dad collected sports cards, comic books, cookbooks, and old letters. Dad was in the army and far away. "Remember Dad's rules," said Mom.

"Rule one is to be gentle," said Nathan. "Rule two is to put things back."

"Those are good rules," said Will. Nathan showed Will some of his dad's coolest stuff. As Mom dusted a nook of the attic, she moved a wooden box. *Nathan's Comic Books* was printed on the box.

"Nathan, you collect stuff too?" asked Will.

"Just comic books," said Nathan. "But I have some good ones."

Nathan took the box down. He showed Will his comic books. Will spotted a comic book that shocked him.

A Brief History of Money

by Tim Borowski
illustrated by Mark Corcoran

Decodable Story 19

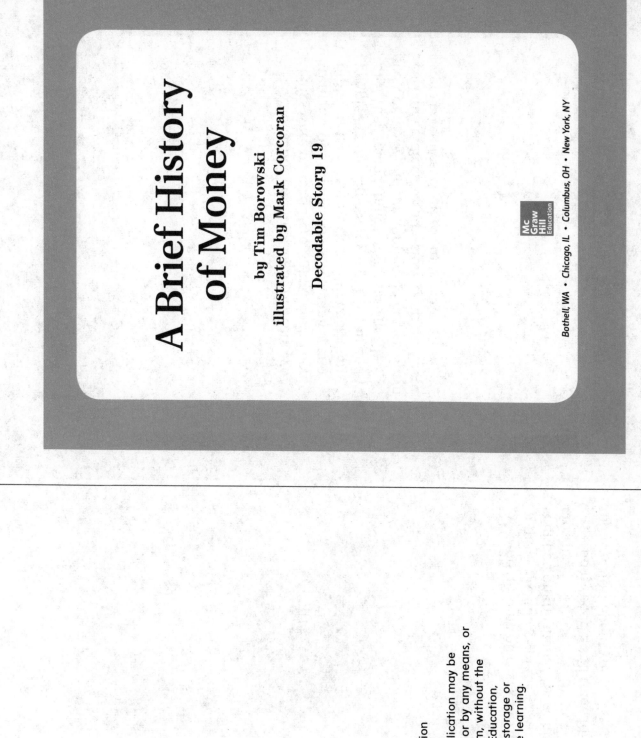

Bothell, WA • Chicago, IL • Columbus, OH • New York, NY

MHEonline.com

Send all inquiries to:
McGraw-Hill Education
8787 Orion Place
Columbus, OH 43240

Thousands and thousands of years ago, things were much different than now. There were no comic books, no video games, and probably no wheat crackers. But back then, people did the same thing that Nathan and Will did. They traded things. If families needed a cow or a bag of flour, they could not set down cash or credit cards on a store counter. There were no stores, cash, or credit cards!

And in some places, kings and queens decided the value of money. Outlines of the crowned kings and queens were stamped on the metal. These bits of metal were called crowns.

Today, people still trade to get things, but most use money. How about you?

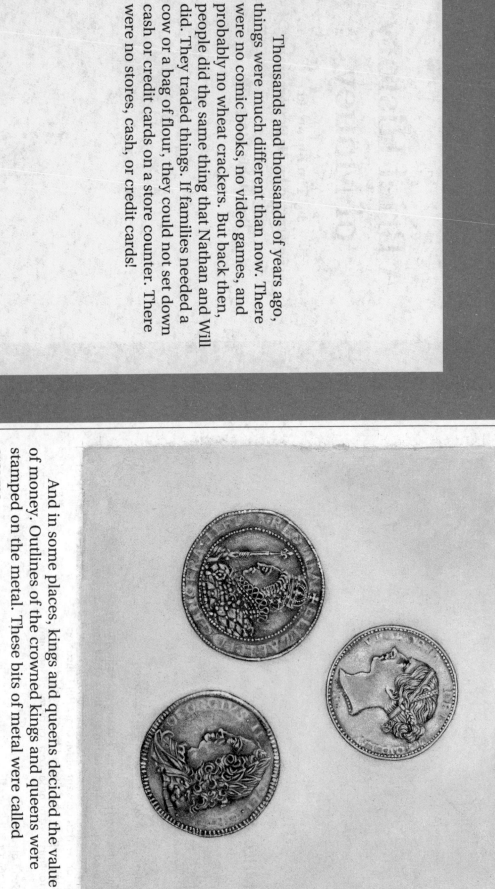

People did not always trade. At one time, humans were hunters and gatherers. They found or hunted enough to survive.

Later, people started raising crops. That may be when trading started. A farm family who had lots of corn, for example, might barter it for things they did not have, such as a cow. Think about the things people may have bartered for thousands of years ago.

Since trading did not work well all the time, a new method for payment was invented. People started to use objects to buy and sell things. These objects became known as money.

At first, money was strange. It might be shells, beads, or other things. But this did not always work well. What was the value of a shell? How many beads were enough to pay for a cow or a bag of flour? Did five or five thousand sound right?

People stopped using shells and beads for money. They started using parts of metal that had real value— gold, silver, or copper.

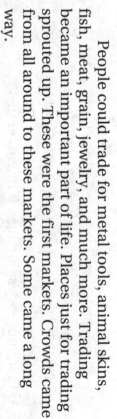

People could trade for metal tools, animal skins, fish, meat, grain, jewelry, and much more. Trading became an important part of life. Places just for trading sprouted up. These were the first markets. Crowds came from all around to these markets. Some came a long way.

The first towns probably grew around these trading markets. Houses, blacksmith shops, and town meeting places surrounded trading markets.

Trading helped people, but there were still problems. Think about it, and you will see why.

What if a farmer had a cow to trade? He would lead it from his farm or house to a market. That might take a long time. Now what if he roamed all over the market and found not one thing he needed? He then had to take the cow back to his farm or house.

Money Stories

by Liam Miller

illustrated by Mark Corcoran

Decodable Story 21

Bothell, WA • Chicago, IL • Columbus, OH • New York, NY

The history of our money is long and has enjoyable twists. A way to learn about that history is to study words we use to talk about money.

The term *money* itself is interesting. Where did it come from?

Buck is short for "buckskin." A buckskin is an animal skin. Long ago, people in the United States used buckskins like money! A real ten bucks would not fit in your pocket. You would need a case—a big, big one!

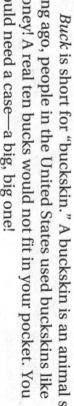

Long ago, there were no banks to keep valuables safe. So where did people keep money? A good choice was to store it in temples.

Temples were like churches. Greeks and Romans made large, safe temples of strong stone.

Temples were also safe places to make money. Coins were made in a well-known Roman temple. Royal faces were stamped on those coins. Soon people thought that this temple's name meant "to make coins."

Over thousands of years, human voices in many places changed the sound of that temple's name.

Two very different words came from that name. The first is *mint*, which means "to make money." The second is *money* itself!

Many other words came from old Rome. *Cent* came from a name that meant "100." *Dime* came from a name that meant "ten." How many cents make a dollar? How many dimes in a dollar?

Dollar did not come from Rome. It came from an old German term for a silver coin used long, long ago. Now, on United States' soil, *dollar* may be the most used of all the money words!

But we also say *cash* a lot. *Cash* came from a French name for a case that held coins.

Not all money words came from other places. Take the term *buck*. We say things like, "I bought this toy for ten bucks."

Salary is an interesting term that came from Rome. You know what *salary* means. It is "pay an employee earns." *Salary* came from an old Roman name for salt.

How did words like *salary* and *salt* ever get joined together in history?

Remember, strange things were used for money long ago. Salt was used for cash back then. Salt was valued highly. It made food taste better. It also kept food safe for a long time. Salt helped Romans store food in winter and on long trips at sea. So in early Roman times, employees did not feel disappointed when they were paid with salt!

Today, would you enjoy getting a bag of salt for mowing a lawn?

116

Seven Bank Facts

by Katherine Burke
illustrated by Mark Corcoran

Decodable Story 22

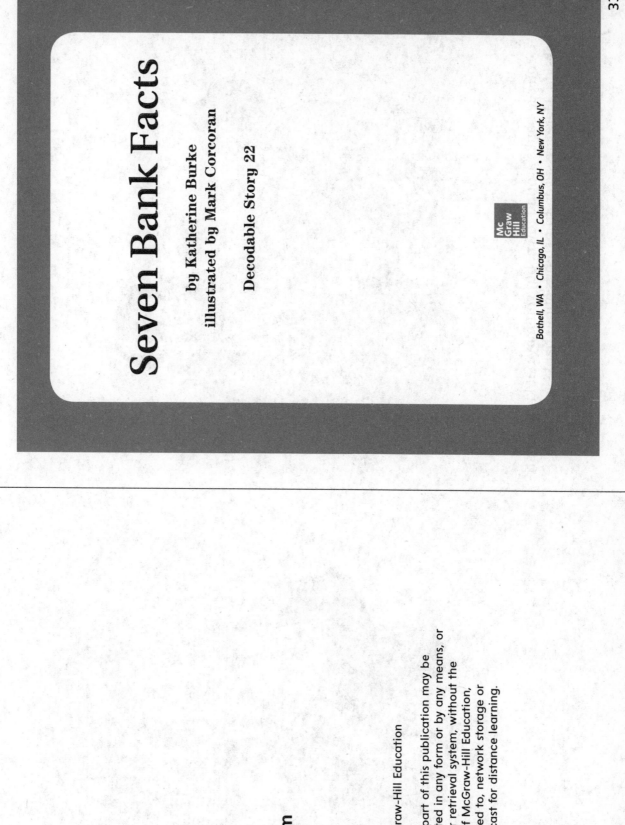

Mc Graw Hill Education

Bothell, WA • Chicago, IL • Columbus, OH • New York, NY

117

You see banks around town, but you may not know what banks do. Here are seven true things about banks.

1. Banks pay you cash.

If you open a savings account for a set time, a bank makes a pledge to you. It will pay you a few cents for each dollar you save in an account. You choose how long you keep the account. The longer you keep it, the bigger it will continue to grow.

2. Banks use your money to make money.

A bank pays you cash because you allow it to use your money. A bank lends it out. People who borrow that cash pledge to pay it back—and add extra cash as they do. That extra cash is known as interest. Some interest pays the few cents per dollar that the bank owes you. The rest is the bank's profit.

6. Banks will count your coins.

Some kids have piggy banks loaded with coins. There may be too many coins to count. Your bank will count them for free.

Banks have fast electronic counting devices. A bank teller scoops coins into the device. The device counts the coins and stacks them in round paper tubes. Those coins you so slowly saved get counted very quickly.

7. Bank accounts are backed up by the United States.

Pretend you had a thousand bucks in a bank account. Is that cash really safe? Yes! It is safe even if your bank runs out of money, burns down, or blows away in a storm. The United States makes bank accounts safe. No matter what happens to the bank, Uncle Sam will hand you back every cent in that account.

Can your piggy bank say that?

119

3. Banks do not keep much cash in their vaults.

Will a bank keep huge stacks of cash around? Nope. It keeps small amounts on hand. But most cash is kept in the form of computer records.

4. Banks use cameras.

Bank cameras zoom in on drive-up windows, ATMs, lobbies, counting rooms, vaults, and even roofs. Cameras follow your every step. Try to look cute for the camera!

5. Banks store more than cash.

Do you own valuable comic books or jewels? Do you own a crown from when your mom was a queen? (Wow!) Do you own gold chains? Where can you safely store these things? Banks rent metal boxes for a low fee. The bank stores these boxes in a fireproof vault.

Bank boxes come in different sizes. A big box will store pounds of salt. So keep mowing!

120

Dad Is Back

by Tim Borowski
illustrated by Lynne Avril

Decodable Story 23

Bothell, WA • Chicago, IL • Columbus, OH • New York, NY

Mc Graw Hill Education

MHEonline.com

Mc Graw Hill Education

Send all inquiries to:
McGraw-Hill Education
8787 Orion Place
Columbus, OH 43240

Nathan's dad came home from the army. The day his dad returned, Nathan was happy and proud. Dad was safe and sound. And Dad looked so cool in his green uniform.

"I sold this drawing to a newspaper for kids. It was your idea," explained Dad.

"Cool," said Nathan. And it was!

Now Dad was going to start a new job. Nathan called Will to tell him all about his dad's new job.

Nathan began by saying, "You know my dad likes cartoons and comic books like the Blue Hood."

"Me too," said Will.

Nathan continued, "Well, my dad's new job is to draw cartoons!"

"Wow!" shouted Will.

The next day, Dad and Nathan walked to the mall for drawing paper. "I have to think of ideas for cartoons," Dad said.

"I'll help!" said Nathan.

"I know you will," smiled Dad.

As they walked, Nathan saw Dad point to an ATM. It was on an outside wall of a drugstore. "Nate, I need to get cash," said Dad.

"That's neat, too!" said Dad. He paused and asked, "And now, Nate, what do you think about ATMs?"

"I know the truth, Dad," said Nathan. "Mom taught me that bank employees load ATMs with cash every day."

Dad grinned. "And my money comes from my bank account."

Dad bought his drawing pads. Then Dad and Nathan walked home. They threw a baseball back and forth. Nathan was happy that Dad was home.

The following week, Dad showed Nathan a drawing. It was called "Which Way Does an ATM Work?" Dad had drawn three cartoons. The first showed tiny people inside an ATM. The second showed tubes running from a bank to ATMs all over town. The third showed bank employees loading cash into an ATM.

Dad slipped a plastic card into the ATM. Then he punched some numbers on the ATM number pad. Soon the ATM was counting out cash. Nathan liked the sound of money counting as it came out of the ATM.

"That is so cool," said Nathan. "When I was little, I thought a few tiny people stood in the ATM and handed out cash for free. Can you believe that?"

Dad smiled. "That would be neat if it were true."

"And when I grew bigger, I had a new idea," said Nathan.

"I expect it was a good one, too," said Dad.

"I thought long tubes ran from the bank to all the ATMs," said Nathan. "I thought the bank had a huge pool of cash. The cash would shoot out smoothly from the pool to the tubes and into ATMs."

Decodable Stories' Table

Getting Started

Lesson	Core Decodable	Practice Decodable	Sound/Spelling Correspondences	High-Frequency Words Introduced
Day 1	1 Matt, Kim, and Sam	1 Sam	/a/ spelled *a* /d/ spelled *d* /h/ spelled *h_* /m/ spelled *m* /n/ spelled *n* /s/ spelled *s, ss* /t/ spelled *t, tt* /i/ spelled *i* /o/ spelled *o* /b/ spelled *b* /k/ spelled *c, k* /f/ spelled *f, ff* /g/ spelled *g*	hand, high, land, watch
Day 2	2 Fast Sam	2 Help	/e/ spelled *e, _ea_* /j/ spelled *j* /l/ spelled *l, ll* /p/ spelled *p* /r/ spelled *r* /ks/ spelled ▪*x* /u/ spelled *u* /kw/ spelled *qu_* /v/ spelled *v* /w/ spelled *w_* /y/ spelled *y_* /z/ spelled *z, zz, _s*	hear, next, still, until
Day 3	3 Midge	3 Fran and Ann	/j/ spelled ▪*dge* /k/ spelled ▪*ck* /ng/ spelled ▪*ng* /nk/ spelled ▪*nk* /a/ spelled *a* /e/ spelled *e, _ea_* /i/ spelled *i* /o/ spelled *o* /u/ spelled *u*	back, children, head, move, plants, second
Day 4	4 Tell Your Pals	4 Fran's Story	/ar/ spelled *ar* /er/ spelled *er, ir, ur, ear* /or/ spelled *or, ore*	earth, hard, last, more, school, story, than
Day 5	5 Stars	5 Fishing	/sh/ spelled *sh* /th/ spelled *th* /ch/ spelled *ch*	above, answer, friend, night, turned

Unit 1

Lesson	Core Decodable	Practice Decodable	Sound/Spelling Correspondences	High-Frequency Words Introduced
Lesson 1	6 Val's New Bike	6 Dave's New Home	/ā/ spelled *a, a_e* /ī/ spelled *i, i_e* /ō/ spelled *o, o_e*	change, find, home, most, talk, thought
Lesson 2	7 Vic's Big Chore	7 Dave Returns	/ē/ spelled *e, e_e* /ū/ spelled *u, u_e*	close, time, while
Lesson 3	8 Gem Is Missing	8 More Clover	/j/ spelled *ge, gi_* /s/ spelled *ce, ci_, cy*	large, name, things
Lesson 4	9 On a Train	9 Riddles	/ā/ spelled *ai_, _ay* /ə/ spelled *_le, _el, _al, _il*	city, each, face, near, through, took
Lesson 5	10 Bike Races	10 Dad Wraps a Gift	/f/ spelled *ph* /m/ spelled *_mb* /n/ spelled *kn_* /r/ spelled *wr_* /w/ spelled *wh_*	almost, also, years
Lesson 6	11 Too Cold?	11 I Was Inside a Dragon	Review Lessons 1–5	air, such

Unit 2

Lesson	Core Decodable	Practice Decodable	Sound/Spelling Correspondences	High-Frequency Words Introduced
Lesson 1	12 The Empty Field	12 Lee's Eagle	/ē/ spelled *ee, ea, _y, _ie_, _ey*	eyes, part
Lesson 2	13 Bats	13 Mack's Problem	/ī/ spelled *_igh, _ie, _y*	even, might, need, trees
Lesson 3	14 More Bats	14 An Old Boat	/ō/ spelled *oa_, _ow*	house, same, side
Lesson 4	15 Condors	15 Mew? Mew?	/ū/ spelled *_ew, _ue*	feet, world, without
Lesson 5	16 A Visit	16 Yikes! Sue!	/o͞o/ spelled *oo, u, u_e, _ew, _ue*	end, should
Lesson 6	17 Migrating Geese	17 Strange Stuff	Review Lessons 1–5	along, began, following

Unit 3

Lesson	Core Decodable	Practice Decodable	Sound/Spelling Correspondences	High-Frequency Words Introduced
Lesson 1	18 A Trade	18 Hockey Tryouts	Contrast /oo/ and /o͞o/ spelled *oo*	book, letters
Lesson 2	19 A Brief History of Money	19 Snow	/ow/ spelled *ow, ou_*; Contrast with /ō/ spelled *_ow*	enough, set
Lesson 3	20 Collecting Baseball Cards	20 The Hawk	/aw/ spelled *au_, aw, augh, ough, al, all*	between, ever
Lesson 4	21 Money Stories	21 Cowboy Roy's Two Rules	/oi/ spelled *oi, _oy*	words
Lesson 5	22 Seven Bank Facts	22 Josh and Brownie	/ō/ spelled *_ow* /ū/ spelled *u_e, _ew, _ue* /o͞o/ spelled *_ue, _ew, u_e* /ow/ spelled *ow*	paper
Lesson 6	23 Dad Is Back	23 A Crew in Outer Space	Review Lessons 1–5	point

Grade 3 High-Frequency Words

above	earth	high	night	than
air	end	home	paper	things
almost	enough	house	part	thought
along	even	land	plants	through
also	ever	large	point	time
answer	eyes	last	same	took
back	face	letters	school	trees
began	feet	might	second	turned
between	find	more	set	until
book	following	most	should	watch
change	friend	move	side	while
children	hand	name	still	without
city	hard	near	story	words
close	head	need	such	world
each	hear	next	talk	years

Grade 2 High-Frequency Words

again	easy	many	people	these
always	eight	may	picture	think
animal	everyone	mouse	piece	those
another	everything	Mr.	please	three
because	far	Mrs.	pull	today
been	few	much	quite	together
believe	first	myself	read	uncle
better	full	never	seven	under
black	give	new	show	upon
both	goes	nine	sign	us
bring	gray	off	small	use
brother	great	often	something	warm
brought	hold	once	soon	wash
buy	horse	only	sorry	which
carry	knew	open	start	white
center	laugh	other	stop	who
circle	learn	ought	taste	why
different	light	our	tell	work
does	listen	own	ten	write
done	live	paste	thank	zero

Grade 1 High-Frequency Words

about	come	how	one	too
after	could	if	or	two
an	day	into	over	very
any	don't	its	pretty	walk
are	every	jump	put	want
around	five	just	red	water
ask	four	know	ride	way
away	from	like	right	well
before	get	long	saw	went
big	going	make	six	where
blue	good	me	sleep	will
brown	got	my	take	would
by	green	no	their	yellow
call	help	now	them	yes
came	here	old	this	your

Grade K High-Frequency Words

a	did	her	on	they
all	do	him	out	to
am	down	his	said	up
and	for	I	see	was
as	girl	in	she	we
at	go	is	some	were
be	had	it	that	what
boy	has	little	the	when
but	have	look	then	with
can	he	of	there	you